Thank You
for Being
My Parents

Other books by

Blue Mountain Press INC

Come Into the Mountains, Dear Friend
by Susan Polis Schutz
I Want to Laugh, I Want to Cry
by Susan Polis Schutz
Peace Flows from the Sky
by Susan Polis Schutz
Someone Else to Love
by Susan Polis Schutz
I'm Not That Kind of Girl
by Susan Polis Schutz
Yours If You Ask
by Susan Polis Schutz
Love, Live and Share
by Susan Polis Schutz
The Language of Friendship
The Language of Love
The Language of Happiness
The Desiderata of Happiness
by Max Ehrmann
I Care About Your Happiness
by Kahlil Gibran/Mary Haskell
I Wish You Good Spaces
Gordon Lightfoot
We Are All Children Searching for Love
by Leonard Nimoy
Come Be with Me
by Leonard Nimoy
These Words Are for You
by Leonard Nimoy
Creeds to Love and Live By
On the Wings of Friendship
You've Got a Friend
Carole King
With You There and Me Here
The Dawn of Friendship
Once Only
by jonivan
Expressing Our Love
Just the Way I Am
Dolly Parton
You and Me Against the World
Paul Williams
Words of Wisdom, Words of Praise
Reach Out for Your Dreams
I Promise You My Love
A Mother's Love
A Friend Forever
gentle freedom, gentle courage
diane westlake
You Are Always My Friend
When We Are Apart
It's Nice to Know Someone Like You
by Peter McWilliams
It Isn't Always Easy
My Sister, My Friend

Thank You for Being My Parents

An anthology of poems on
parents, love and family

Edited by Susan Polis Schutz

Blue Mountain Press ™

Boulder, Colorado

Library of Congress Number: 80-70743
ISBN: 0-88396-137-7

Manufactured in the United States of America
First Printing: March, 1981
Second Printing: April, 1982

The following works have previously appeared in Blue Mountain Arts publications:
"To Mom," by Miles M. Hutchinson. "There is nothing more wonderful," by J. Russell Morrison. "My trust for you," by Susan Polis Schutz. "To Dad," by Andrew Harding Allen. Copyright © Continental Publications, 1979. "Since I have a mother," by Susan Polis Schutz. Copyright © Continental Publications, 1973. "Knowing that you," by Susan Polis Schutz. Copyright © Continental Publications, 1972. "When someone cares," by Susan Polis Schutz. Copyright © Continental Publications, 1974. "Thinking of home," by Louise Bradford Lowell. Copyright © Continental Publications, 1978. "A Mother's Love," by Debra Colin-Cooke. Copyright © Debra Colin-Cooke, 1980. "The love of a family," by Susan Polis Schutz. Copyright © Stephen Schutz and Susan Polis Schutz, 1980. "We have something special," "Because of you, Dad," "For all you have done," and "To My Father," by Andrew Tawney. Copyright © Blue Mountain Arts, Inc., 1980. "A family's feelings," by Jamie Delere. "Our family," by Andrew Tawney. Copyright © Blue Mountain Arts, Inc., 1981.
"A father's love," by Ruth Langdon Morgan. Copyright © Ruth Langdon Morgan, 1980. All rights reserved.

Thanks to the Blue Mountain Arts creative staff, with special thanks to Jody Cone.

ACKNOWLEDGMENTS are on page 63

Blue Mountain Press INC.

P.O. Box 4549, Boulder, Colorado 80306

Contents

Both of You—My Parents

It would take
forever to say my thanks
    you've given me more than I can repay
    you've given me love . . . you gave me life
    you stood by me through weary days
Throughout my life when I was weak
    there you were to help me along
    through all my hardships and periods of doubt
    your support made me strong
I couldn't tell you how much it means
    just to know that you're around
    things are richer when shared with you
    you fill my ups and comfort my downs

When things are happy—I come to you
you listen intently with such concern
I feel important that you should care
no matter how trivial—you help me learn
When things are bad—I come to you
you share with me the wisdom of years
experience helps you solve my problems
but love is how you solve my fears
I'm sorry I often take you for granted
but I love you dearly—I really do
in all the earth there's nothing worth having
compared to the love
of both of you . . . my parents

—James Bruce Joseph Sievers

To Mom

Thanks for listening
Thanks for caring
Thanks for always helping
in times of need
Thanks for sharing
Thanks, Mom
for always being there

—Miles M. Hutchinson

To Dad

*We have something special
that no one
   no distance
      no time
   can take away . . .
we have each other.*

—Andrew Tawney

*The love
of a family
is so
uplifting.*

*The warmth
of a family
is so
comforting.*

*The support
of a family
is so reassuring.*

*The attitude
of a family
towards
each other
molds one's
attitude forever
towards the
world.*

—Susan Polis Schutz

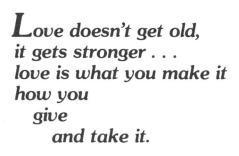

*Love doesn't get old,
it gets stronger . . .
love is what you make it
how you
    give
        and take it.*

—*Paul Williams*

*Thank you for your
presence in my life . . .
you encourage me to go
beyond myself.*

—*Linda DuPuy Moore*

Thank you for being my parents
Thank you for the love you have shown me
Thank you for the protection you have given me
Thank you for the guidance you have provided
Thank you for the truth you have taught me
Thank you for the values you have demonstrated
Thank you for being my family.

—Susan Polis Schutz

My Mother

Throughout our lives as we count our successes and pat ourselves on the back, how seldom do we remember who it was that began it all. I was very fortunate in God's decision that I be given to the woman I now know as my mother, for it was she who showed me how to care, how to love, how to feel, and how to be free.

—James Bruce Joseph Sievers

My Dad

Many men are strong, but very
few have been able to mix the
right amount of strength with a
proportionate amount of gentleness.
In doing so, you get a man you can
admire, respect, and look up to,
but also a man you can talk to
who will understand and listen.
All my life my father has given me a
feeling of security. No matter where
I go or what happens to me, I've always
known he's been back there watching
patiently should I need him. This
security has given me the strength to
stand on my own many times.

—James Bruce Joseph Sievers

Parents' Creed

And a woman who held a babe against her bosom said: Speak to us of Children. And he said: your children are not your children. They are the sons and daughters of life's longing for itself. They come through you but not from you, and though they are with you, they belong not to you. You may give them your love but not your thoughts, for they have their own thoughts. You may house their bodies but not their souls, for their souls dwell in the house of tomorrow, which you cannot visit, not even in your dreams. You may strive to be like them, but seek not to make them like you. For life goes not backward nor tarries with yesterday. You are the bows from which your children as living arrows are sent forth.

—Kahlil Gibran

*There is nothing more wonderful
in the world
than the feeling
you get from sharing,
and there is no greater happiness
than the warmth
you get from loving.*

—J. Russell Morrison

A Mother's Love

A special kind of love that's always there when you need it to comfort and inspire, yet lets you go your own path. A sharing heart filled with patience and forgiveness, that takes your side even when wrong. Nothing can take its place.

—Debra Colin-Cooke

For all you have done
　　for the gifts you have given
For the love you have shown
　　in the life we are living . . .

I thank you with the whole
of my heart.

—Andrew Tawney

Since I have a mother
whose many interests
keep her excited and occupied

Since I have a mother
who interacts with so many people
that she has a real feeling for
the world

Since I have a mother
who always is strong
through any period of suffering

Since I have a mother
who is a complete person
I always have a model
to look up to
and that makes it easier
for me to develop into
an independent person
Thanks, Mom

—Susan Polis Schutz

Because of you, Dad

Because of you I've come to experience an endearment to life and living, to love and to all that speaks of home.

For the affinity of father and child is a special union; a sacred and holy tie, a natural and earthly bond.

You have helped to raise and guide me through infancy and youth, from sapling to sturdy oak.

Together we are like a green and growing tree, nourished by the love of our immediate family and by our fathers' spirits before us.

Each year we grow stronger and yet more supple, able to bend without breaking and stand firm without faltering.

Our visible growth is easily perceived with each passage of time, but the union of father and child extends far beyond outward appearance and apparent change.

For in our quest for new heights—our ever-reaching branches against the sky—we have also grown deep and interwoven roots.

Together we share a common ground, and we take pride in our commitment.

Our love is a treasure that continues to increase—ever evolving to the eye; experienced ever deeper by the heart.

Surely, our companionship is a wondrous element of nature's design.

Out of the harvest of life, we will reap the rewards of family love and continuing contentment. A union such as ours will always weather the changing seasons.

*I have realized a fine and full existence...
because of you, Dad.*

—Andrew Tawney

To My Parents

When I was young
and learning to dream,
you were always there
you listened . . . and encouraged
me to follow
my dreams.
You helped me to become
all that I am.
Because you believed in me
I learned to believe
in myself.
Thank you for everything.

—Linda DuPuy Moore

*Many make the household
but only one the home.*

—James Russell Lowell

Mother

You formed my life . . . with your own,
and you taught me sensitivity and loyalty,
　　how to love
　　　　and to give.
You inspired my dreams and ambitions,
　helping me along the way.

You've always been there, Mom,
　　and I love you.

—Teresa M. Fox

My Parents

You are
so loving
so giving
so caring
so special—
I thank God
that I was
born
to
you

—Susan Polis Schutz

Thinking of home
Thinking of the past
Thinking of tomorrow
Brings me closer to you
You are a special person
who brings lasting joy
into my life

—*Louise Bradford Lowell*

My sentiments remain the same . . . the feeling of thanks for that grand love of yours towards your child, which you displayed so warmly and so tenderly.

—Richard Wagner

My trust for you is so complete
You can advise me
You can yell at me
You can be honest with me
But please always tell me
whatever you are thinking
I respect your opinion on
    everything
as I respect the way you think
and the way you are

—Susan Polis Schutz

*K*nowing that you are always
here to understand and
accept me helps me get along
in the confused world. If
every person could have
someone just like you, the
world would become a
peaceful garden.

—Susan Polis Schutz

*The best and most beautiful
things in the world
cannot be seen
or even touched.
They must be felt
with the heart.*

—*Helen Keller*

While a child is growing up, a mother gives her love, strength, time, devotion, wisdom and protection to that child. When the child turns into an adult, a mother releases, so the adult can learn and use the mother's wisdom in daily situations, while drawing strength from her to be a part of the world.

But the mother's love is never forgotten or replaced. A mother's love and understanding are always there, as it was in the beginning . . . and will always be, forever.

—Cheryl Lynn Jackson

A family's feelings
for each other
provide strength and comfort
even on the cloudiest of days.

—*Jamie Delere*

each day and night
  i feel your presence
you may not be near to touch
but you are in my mind and heart
you meet my needs so silently
i am not alone because of you

—diane westlake

We are becoming
more understanding
of each other's needs
This is good;
for we must always keep
some of our needs
independent in order
to maintain our own identities
It is even better
that we can have these things
in ourselves
and still at all times
have each other

—jonivan

You have loved me
and nurtured me
through many years,
and I have
cherished no others
so much.
Home is always with you,
wherever
you may be.

—jonivan

When someone cares
it is easier to speak
it is easier to listen
it is easier to play
it is easier to work

When someone cares
it is easier to laugh

—Susan Polis Schutz

A Mother's Heart

A mother's heart
holds the fondest memories
and the noblest dreams
for her child.
I am grateful when
I think of
your loving heart, Mother.
Thanks for letting go
yet clasping me
always
to your loving heart.

—Jean Therese Lynch

A father's love
is a special kind
of love
that's always there
when you need it
to comfort and inspire.
It lets you go
your own way.

—Ruth Langdon Morgan

To My Father

My prayer is that I may pass along to my own children as much nourishment of the soul and as much fulfillment of the heart as you have given me.

—*Andrew Tawney*

*P*arents are very special people—
    to each other
       and to their children.
Through the years
    you have shown this to me
By giving me love
    by always being there.
Whether it be
    to comfort me in times of need
    or to share with me my happiness.
It is such a special feeling
    to know that I do have parents
      as wonderful as the two of you
    whom I love and respect so very much.
And yet . . .

MɑD 5/11/85

because feelings are so very hard
    to put into words
I don't tell you often enough
    how very much I do love you
and how very much I really do need you.
And I don't
    thank you often enough
    for being—
        the two beautiful parents
    that you have been to me.
So on this day
    on this very special day
        I would just like to say
    that yes—
Parents are very special people—
    and none could ever—
        be as beautiful—
    as the two of you are to me.
Mom and Dad—
    I love you.

                    —Karen Meditz

There are so many times
I think of you
and want to thank you
for the wonderful moments
we've shared
and the happiness we've felt.

I love you both,
and this seemed
like a nice moment
to tell you.

—Jan Kirkley Boyd

for the people in your life . . .
    if you miss them
    tell them
    when you think of them
    let them know

—diane westlake

Our family

*Our feelings of closeness
will never be limited
by the time we spend apart.
Homes and families
as precious as ours
can only be comprised of
   near and caring feelings.
Our family is such an essential part
   of our lives,
that the caring will never leave
      the home,
and the love will reside
         continually in the heart.*

—*Andrew Tawney*

Mother, You Touch Everything I Do

Mother, you have always
been a model for me—
your wonderful ways
touching everything I do.
Your constant love and kindness
have been the source of my joy
and have enabled me
to share my happiness with others.
From you I have learned patience,
as you have been unselfish
with your time,
listening thoughtfully to all of my problems.
Your sensitive understanding
    of my many moods
has carried me through the darkest hours
of sadness and desperation
You have always been
a bright sun shining
on a cloudy day.
I thank you for your
caring guidance—
It has allowed me to fully
appreciate the joy of living.
My hope is to live my life
as you have done—
a life of loving inspiration.

—E. Lori Milton

To Dad

You have always been there when I needed you. Even though we don't always agree with each other, our love has always prevailed. You have taught me kindness and understanding—you have given me the ability to find love in the world.

—Andrew Harding Allen

A Mother . . .

More than a woman, she's your
   dearest friend,
always there when no one else is around,
always giving of herself,
   and giving her all.

Someone that will never laugh
   at your mistakes,
for your hurt becomes hers.
Always standing beside you,
never in front or behind you.
As strong as an oak tree,
yet as gentle as a morning rainfall
and as beautiful as a sunset;
everlasting beauty that will never perish,
My mother . . . I love her so.

—Cynthia Smith Medina

To my parents

*I am more than proud
to be your daughter.
I am more than proud
to love you.*

—*Susan Polis Schutz*

Acknowledgments

We gratefully acknowledge the permission granted by the following authors, publishers and authors' representatives to reprint poems and excerpts from their publications.

Starboard Publishing Company for "Both of You, My Parents," "My Dad" and "My Mother," by James Bruce Joseph Sievers. Copyright © Starboard Publishing Company, 1976. All rights reserved. Reprinted by permission.

Warner Bros. Music for "Love doesn't get old," by Paul Williams. From the song "LOVE CONQUERS ALL," lyrics by Paul Williams. Copyright © 1977 WB Music Corp. All rights reserved. Reprinted by permission.

Alfred A. Knopf, Inc. for "Parents Creed," by Kahlil Gibran. From THE PROPHET by Kahlil Gibran. Copyright © 1923 by Kahlil Gibran. Copyright renewed 1951 by Administrators C.T.A. of Kahlil Gibran Estate, and Mary G. Gibran. Reprinted by permission of Alfred A. Knopf, Inc. All rights reserved.

Diane Westlake for "each day and night." Copyright © Diane Westlake, 1977. And for "for the people in your life . . ." Copyright © Diane Westlake, 1978. All rights reserved. Reprinted by permission.

jonivan for "We are becoming" and "My Parents." Copyright © jonivan, 1980. All rights reserved. Reprinted by permission.

Linda DuPuy Moore for "Thank you" and "To My Parents." Copyright © Linda DuPuy Moore, 1980. All rights reserved. Reprinted by permission.

Cheryl Lynn Jackson for "While a child is growing up." Copyright © Cheryl Lynn Jackson, 1980. All rights reserved. Reprinted by permission.

Teresa M. Fox for "Mother." Copyright © Teresa M. Fox, 1980. All rights reserved. Reprinted by permission.

Jean Therese Lynch for "A Mother's Heart." Copyright © Jean Therese Lynch, 1980. All rights reserved. Reprinted by permission.

Jan Kirkley Boyd for "There are so many times." Copyright © Jan Kirkley Boyd, 1980. All rights reserved. Reprinted by permission.

E. Lori Milton for "Mother, You Touch Everything I Do," by E. Lori Milton. Copyright © E. Lori Milton, 1981. All rights reserved. Reprinted by permission.

Cynthia Smith Medina for "A Mother." Copyright © Cynthia Smith Medina, 1981. All rights reserved. Reprinted by permission.

Karen Meditz for "Parents are very special people." Copyright © Karen Meditz, 1981. All rights reserved. Reprinted by permission.

A careful effort has been made to trace the ownership of poems used in this anthology in order to obtain permission to reprint copyrighted material and to give proper credit to the copyright owners.

If any error or omission has occurred, it is completely inadvertent, and we would like to make corrections in future editions provided that written notification is made to the publisher: BLUE MOUNTAIN PRESS, INC., P.O. Box 4549, Boulder, Colorado 80306.